THE WOR[ ]
GUIDE
SELF-DE[ ]

Although this book was written specifically for women, husbands and friends can also obtain knowledge from it. Line drawings, uncluttered, and in black and white, prevail throughout the book, so that the illustrations can be easily viewed and understood. Rather than devoting the time demonstrating natural weapons and the proper defensive blocks, they have been incorporated directly into the techniques. Not only will this book be easy to follow and learn from, but the techniques have been so designed that many of the basic blocks and strikes can be interchangeable, thus conveying the flexibility of the techniques. With this element of flexibility, the student will not be limited only to the approach shown. These techniques were specifically designated by the author, Ed Parker, so that women can apply many of them without using a great deal of strength. However, the effective application of these techniques will still bring about maximum results.

Website address: edparkersr.com

THE WOMAN'S GUIDE TO SELF-DEFENSE

Instruction by Ed Parker Illustrated by Jim McQuade

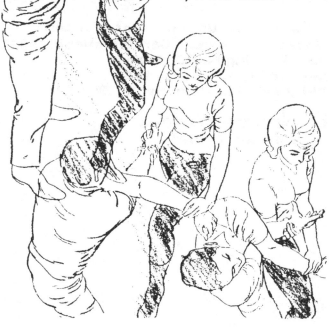

Copyright © 1968 & 2013 by Edmund K. Parker Sr. / Kam IV, Inc.
Preserving the Legacy and Integrity of Edmund K. Parker Sr.
Website address: edparkersr.com

All Rights Reserved. No part of this publication may be reproduced or transmitted in any form or by any means, electronic or mechanical, including photocopy, recording, or any information storage and retrieval system without the written permission of the author.

Printed in the United States of America
Library of Congress Card Number Pending
First Printing March, 1968
Second Printing June, 1988
Third Printing January, 2013

DELSBY PUBLICATIONS
Los Angeles, California

DEDICATION

I dedicate this book to the two most influential, inspiring and encouraging women in my life—my mother and my wife.

TABLE OF CONTENTS

I   Introduction 6
II Anatomical Chart 7
III Natural Weapons 12
IV Contributing Factors in Increasing Force And Effectiveness 17
V   Course I — Techniques Against An Unarmed Attack 18
    A. Two methods of releasing wrist grabs 18
    B. Counter to a grab around the waist while seated 20
    C. Counter to a grab around the waist while standing 22
    D. Counter to a grab from the rear 24
VI Course II — Techniques Against An Unarmed Attack 26
    A. Counter to a front bear hug 26
    B. Counter to a rear bear hug 28
    C. Counter to a front strangle 30
    D. Counter to a rear strangle 33
    E. Counter to a rear forearm choke 38
    F. Counter to a front lapel grab 41
    G. Counter to a front two-hand lapel grab 42
    H. Counter to a hammerlock 44
VII Course III — Techniques Against An Armed Attack 48
    A. Counter to an overhead club 48
    B. Counter to a hooking club 50
    C. Counter to an overhead knife 51
    D. Counter to an underhand knife thrust 53
    E. Counter to a front strangle with a scarf 55
    F. Counter to a rear strangle with a scarf 57
VIII Course IV — Use Of Personal And/Or Household
       Articles As Weapons 59
    A. How to use a tube of lipstick 59
    B. How to use a comb 59
    C. How to use an umbrella 60
    D. How to use a broom or staff 63
IX Course V — Useful Techniques From Unusual Positions   67
    A. How to counter an attack while lying on your stomach 67
    B. How to counter an attack while lying on your back 69
    C. How to counter an attack while lying on your back (variation) 71
    D. How to counter from a kneeling position 73
    E. How to counter from a sitting position 75
X   Helpful Hints And Conclusion 77

I INTRODUCTION

This book was written to provide an uncomplicated but effective means of self-defense suitable for women. Although this book was not written to give complete answers to every conceivable predicament, it will be a useful women's guide to self-defense. It must, however, be emphasized that the best defense is prevention. The techniques illustrated are only useful with practice and understanding, and your knowledge should only be applied when there is no means of escape. Even then, be vicious, striking hard and fast.

It is quite apparent that there is a growing crime rate, juvenile delinquency and high incidence of muggings and sex crimes. Thus, the author felt the need for a realistic method of defense for the cornered woman—the woman who has no means of escape or foreknowledge of an attack. The foregoing techniques were specifically designed for this purpose. While the techniques shown are based on the centuries-old art of Karate, they have been modified for the use of today's modern woman. All of the techniques shown may be learned and practiced alone or with a partner in the privacy of the student's own room. This practice can in no way disfigure the hands or any other part of the body and does not involve hardening or developing parts of the body to adapt them as weapons. Practice is perfectly safe for the student, but while using a partner, one should practice caution. In addition to their use for self-defense, techniques are a healthful form of calisthenics for figure control.

Although the most common types of attacks were chosen to demonstrate defenses against, the student is by no means limited to performing an exact repetition of the techniques shown. These techniques have been so designed that many of the blocking and countering portions can be interchanged so that once they are learned, many variations are possible to fit the situation. No one is able to predict the exact circumstances of an attack and the student may have to deviate slightly from the technique if the situation warrants it. But when armed with the knowledge provided by this book, the student is not prone to panic in time of an emergency and is able to adequately protect herself. It is emphasized that practice is the key to rendering the techniques fully effective.

II ANATOMICAL CHART

A brief study of human anatomy is essential for every woman. Even general knowledge of the location of some of the major nerve centers and critical areas can determine the student's victory or defeat. Such points when struck with your own natural set of weapons can cause paralysis, unconsciousness, extreme pain, or death. In many cases, minimum force applied to the right area can fell an opponent. Many of the principles in this book are based upon the principle of a pin or a nail where the force of the blow is more concentrated so that damage is felt internally as well as externally. For example, if a female was to strike the temple of an opponent with her elbow, and upon contact rendered 80 lbs. of force as compared to a male who might render 160 lbs. of force, her concentrated force would be more than adequate, since only 40 lbs. of force was necessary to down her opponent. No matter how much force is delivered, anything over and above 40 lbs. of force would have been more than ample.

The illustrated anatomical charts, Figs. 1 & 2, are full-length, and display both front and rear views. Only the most vulnerable points on the human body are shown. Points marked with an X are major targets and those marked with an O are secondary targets. There are more points, but these points require considerably more skill to strike effectively. It must be remembered that some of these vital points can never be developed to resist pain or injury.

It is suggested that the student refer to the illustrations and charts as she progresses, and commit them to memory.

Charts 1a and 2a mention the vital points of Figs. 1 & 2, the various methods of attacking these points and the effect they may have on an opponent. Only the practical weapons for women are listed under methods of attack—all others have been left out intentionally. It must be emphasized that some of the weapons mentioned in striking the vital points are only useful depending upon the position and height of the target or the position and height of the one delivering the strikes. Other illustrations will help to clarify this point.

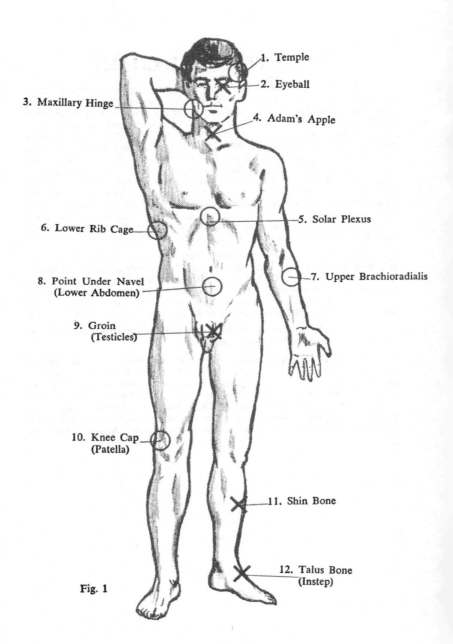

Fig. 1

Accompanying Chart to Fig. 1

VITAL POINTS	METHODS OF ATTACK	EFFECT
1. Temple	Heel of palm, handsword, fist, knee, back fist, hammerfist, elbow, foot	Pain, headache, possible unconsciousness, possible bone fracture or death
2. Eyeball	Finger thrusts (all methods), hooks, claws, slices, whips, etc.	Temporary or permanent loss of eyesight, possible loss of eyeball
3. Maxillary Hinge	Same as (1)	Possible unconsciousness and dislocation
4. Adam's Apple	Half fist, handsword, elbow, footsword	Severe pain, paralysis, loss of speech, physical collapse, gagging and nausea, possible death
5. Solar Plexus	Same as (1)	Temporary paralysis, nausea, physical collapse, possible death
6. Lower Rib Cage	Same as (1)	Pain, possible fracture
7. Upper Brachioradialis	Hammerfist, handsword	Pain, temporary paralysis
8. Point Under Navel	Same as (1)	Loss of breath, possible hemorrhage or death
9. Groin (testicles)	Fist, hammerfist or handsword, reverse hammerfist or handsword, knee, foot (various ways)	Severe pain, paralysis, collapse, possible death
10. Knee Cap	Foot (various methods of)	Pain, unable to stand or walk, possible fracture or dislocation
11. Shin Bone	Hammerfist, foot (various methods of)	Pain, unable to stand or walk, possible fracture
12. Talus Bone	Foot (parts of the heel)	Same as (11)

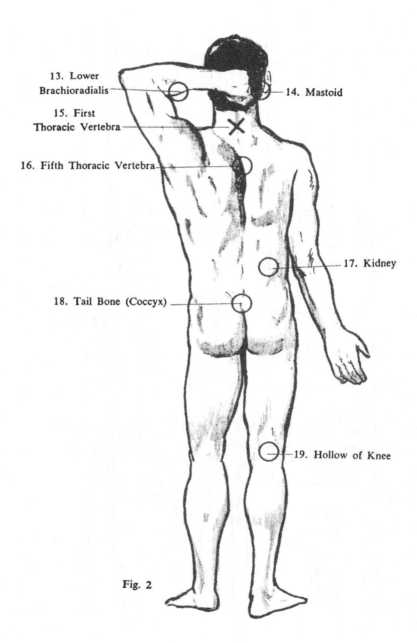

Fig. 2

Accompanying Chart to Fig. 2

VITAL POINTS	METHODS OF ATTACK	EFFECT
13. Lower Brachioradialis	Hammerfist, handsword	Pain, temporary paralysis
14. Mastoid	Fist, hammerfist, handsword, elbow, foot (various ways or parts of)	Pain, headache, possible unconsciousness and fracture, temporary disability
15. First Thoracic Vertebra	Fist, hammerfist, handsword, elbow, knee, foot (various methods of)	Stunning pain, severe headache, possible unconsciousness or death
16. Fifth Thoracic Vertebra	Fist, back fist, hammerfist, heel of palm, elbow, knee, foot (various methods)	Possible paralysis or fracture
17. Kidney	Same as (16)	Severe pain, temporary paralysis, physical collapse, possible rupture
18. Tail Bone	Same as (15)	Severe pain, possible paralysis or fracture
19. Hollow of Knee	Hammerfist, foot (various methods)	Paralysis to lower limb

III NATURAL WEAPONS

The human body contains many natural weapons which can be used effectively and without any development whatever. While it is true that the effectiveness of a developed hand or foot is greater among professional karateists, such development is not essential for effective self-defense. Knowledge of your natural body weapons coupled with a knowledge of your opponent's weak points, as discussed earlier, can produce a variety of effects as indicated by the accompanying charts to Figs. 1 & 2. Then, too, aside from what constitutes our natural weapons and how they can be formed, speed and accuracy must accompany every effort. The effect desired depends upon several factors; namely, the force of the blow (which is proportionate to its speed), the vital area struck and the choice of natural weapons used.

Although there are a vast number of weapons which can be employed, this book will only touch upon those which will be most effective for the female student. The following illustrations are devoted to showing the student some of the natural weapons available. The use of the knee and elbow are highly effective but are not illustrated in this section. They will be employed in many of the techniques in other sections. Likewise many of the blocks and parries used in deflecting and redirecting an opponent's punch or kick will not be treated separately. They are incorporated into the techniques you are about to learn.

The following illustrations are two of the basic kicks you will employ throughout the book. Other types of kicks are incorporated in the techniques themselves and will be explained under their respective illustrations.

SNAPPING FRONT KICK

Figure 3a. Lift your right knee to the level of your waistline or slightly higher. For practice purposes, keep both hands on your hips, keeping your back back straight and head erect. Keep your supporting leg (left leg) bent and flexible, and foot flat. Tightly lock the calf and thigh of your right leg.

Figure 3b. Kick forward with the ball of your right foot, straightening both your knee and ankle at the height of your kick. Your supporting leg (left leg) should still remain bent and your left foot flat. Retrieve your right foot and place it in the identical position as Figure 3a. You may then plant your right foot and proceed again.

NOTE: When kicking or striking, always retrieve faster than delivering an attack. As an example, if your delivery speed is 100 mph, then the retrieving speed should be 110 mph.

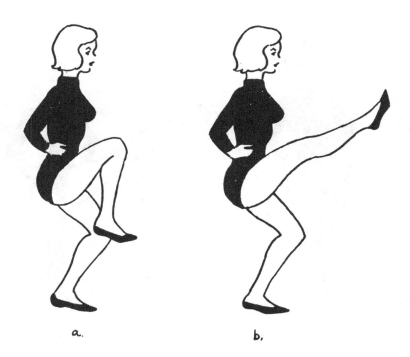

a. b.

Fig. 3

SNAPPING SIDE KICK

Figure 4a. Lift your right knee to the level of your waistline or slightly higher as you cock the right inside portion of the heel against your left inner knee. Keep your hands on your hips, back straight and head erect. Your supporting leg (left leg) again is bent and flexible, with the left foot flat.

Figure 4b. Kick to the side with the bottom or side of the right heel. For more power, throw your right hip into the action by pivoting slightly counter clockwise on the left foot. Your supporting leg should still remain bent and your left foot flat. After fully extending your leg to the side, retrieve your right foot back to the identical position as Figure 4a. You may then plant your right foot and proceed again.

NOTE: The number of repetitions done per type of kick per leg should be graduated. Commence with five kicks per leg and work up to twenty-five or thirty. DO NOT OVERDO any of the above kicks.

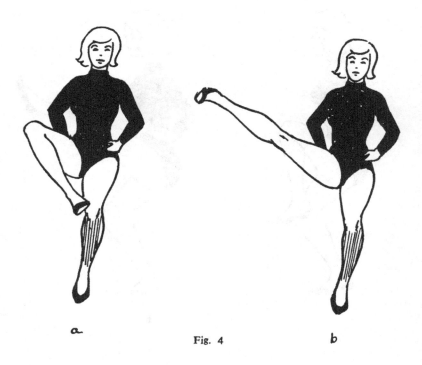

Fig. 4

Figure 5. This illustration shows how to form the hand into two useful natural weapons—the handsword and the half fist. Most men have their fingers extended and close together when using the handsword (side of palm) to chop with. However, it is highly recommended that the student hold her hand in the manner shown. Utilizing this formation will give you a more compact weapon and will help you to strike with greater impact when using the handsword to chop with. The half fist (joints of the fingers) could be used palm up to strike to the Adam's apple.

Figure 6. The half fist is shown again used in a thrusting manner to the Adam's apple striking the target with the palm facing the ground.

Fig. 5   Fig. 6

Figure 7. This is the two finger thrust used mainly to strike the eyeballs.

Figure 8. Again two portions of this hand formation could be used as natural weapons—the hammerfist and the natural fist or forefist. The hammerfist utilizes the same portion of the hand as the handsword with one modification; the hand is tightly clenched upon contact. The forefist could be used to punch with.

Figure 9. This shows another view of the natural fist or forefist and the hammerfist which could be used to strike horizontally in an outward manner as compared to Figure 8 which could be used in a vertical and downward fashion.

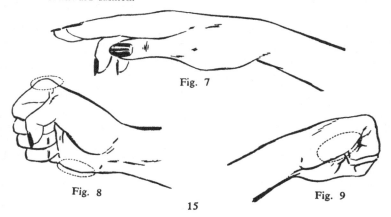

Fig. 7

Fig. 8   Fig. 9

Figure 10. This depicts the heel of the palm which could be used to thrust up against a chin or strike down against the bridge of the opponent's nose.

Figure 11. The five finger claw is mainly used to claw the eyes and face. It can be used to strike from all angles.

Figure 12. This is the five finger whip. A fast whip to the eyes can cause momentary blindness thus allowing you more time to escape or to use your shoes, purse, etc. as weapons.

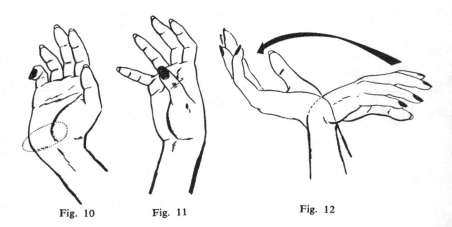

Fig. 10   Fig. 11   Fig. 12

IV CONTRIBUTING FACTORS IN INCREASING FORCE AND EFFECTIVENESS

There are other contributing factors which help to increase force and effectiveness. To assume that striking vital areas alone will do the job is unrealistic. A female student should be made to realize that maximum effectiveness is needed to reassure her of a victory. Hitting a vital area with only 70% effectiveness may do the job in some cases; however, this does not mean that it will work in all cases. A female student should always try to work toward 100% effectiveness to minimize the odds against her. Through constant practice she will realize subtleness and balance. Once balance becomes inherent, force and power automatically increase. To further increase your force, other contributing factors must be considered. How to pivot your body, shuffle and drop your weight with your action so that gravity assists you, or borrow the force or momentum of your opponent, all contribute to maximum effectiveness. These points will be elaborated upon further in explaining the techniques throughout the book.

Continuity and economy of motion are topics also due consideration. Continuity means to have one action flow into another without hesitating or losing motion. In a sense, continuity does entail economy of motion—that is, no wasted motion. When action is taken from whatever state or position you're in, that is economy of motion. In other words, when your first action is used to make contact thus eliminating any telegraphing motion, we can consider this economy of motion. To cause two strikes with one action causing pain or injury to two areas of an opponent with one action is economy of motion. Again this will be pointed out in the techniques that will follow.

V TECHNIQUES

COURSE I — (UNARMED ATTACK)

This course is devoted entirely to ways of discouraging unwanted advances by mashers or other annoying persons. The techniques shown, while painful to the aggressor are not permanently injurious.

A — TWO METHODS OF RELEASING A WRIST GRAB

Figure 13. Shows opponent's left hand grabbing your right wrist.

Figure 14. Release grab by pushing your wrist down and against the index finger, pulling the top of your wrist against the opponent's thumb and toward you. If both your wrists are grabbed, the action is simply doubled.

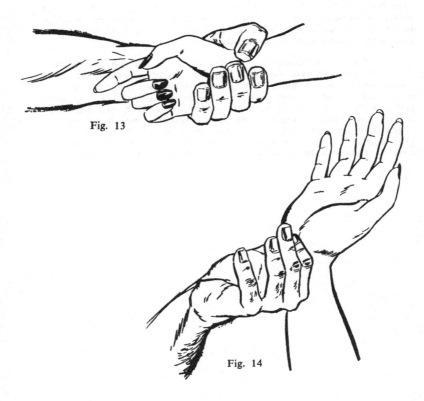

Fig. 13

Fig. 14

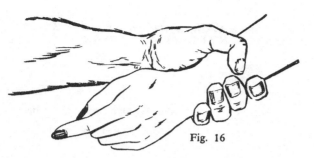

Fig. 16. Opponent's left hand grabs your left wrist.

Fig. 17. Counter grab opponent's left wrist with your left hand.

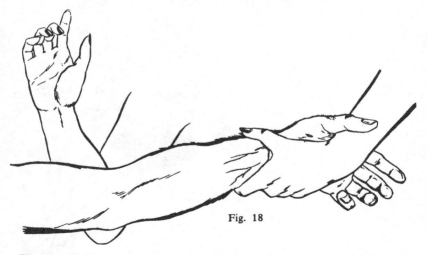

Fig. -18. Pull it toward you with your left hand and strike opponent's left elbow with your right forearm to effect the release.

B — COUNTER TO A GRAB AROUND THE WAIST WHILE SEATED
(COULD BE IN AN AUTO OR ON A COUCH)

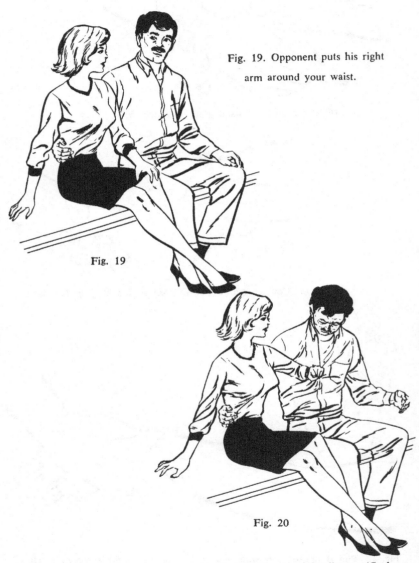

Fig. 19. Opponent puts his right arm around your waist.

Fig. 19

Fig. 20

Fig. 20. Strike opponent's ribs or solar-plexis with your left elbow. (Cock your arm before striking, for added force.)

Fig. 21. Whip the back of your left fingertips to opponent's eyes. (The flick could be just a slap.)

C — COUNTER TO A GRAB AROUND THE WAIST WHILE STANDING
(ARMS ARE FREE)

Fig. 22   Fig. 23

Fig. 22. Both arms of opponent grab you from the front while your arms are free.

Fig. 23. Drop back with your right foot (which places you in better balance) as your left hand grabs your opponent's hair and pulls forward to open up the throat area, simultaneously cock your right hand in the manner illustrated, forming your right hand into a half-fist.

Fig. 24

Fig. 24. Thrust your half-fist to opponent's Adam's apple. The right heel of your palm could be substituted if you should desire to lessen the effect of the blow.

D — COUNTER TO A GRAB FROM THE REAR
(WITH BOTH ARMS PINNED)

Fig. 25

Fig. 26

Fig. 27

Fig. 25 Opponent grabs you from the rear pinning both of your arms above the elbows.

Fig. 26 With your left heel stomp to opponent's right instep.

Fig. 27. Slip your left foot around and behind of your opponent's right leg and cock your left arm.

Fig. 28

Fig. 29

Fig. 28. Pivot to your left and bury your left elbow into opponent's solar-plexis. (Elbow could be directed to opponent's jaw if desired.)

Fig. 29. Pivot even further to your left and deliver a right heel of palm to opponent's chin.

VI TECHNIQUES

COURSE II — (UNARMED ATTACK)

In this course we will advance into serious defensive methods. The defense counters against grabs, chokes, etc. are thoroughly treated. In addition to demonstrating how to break the hold, a sequel of effective counter moves are elaborated upon. Many of these moves can be utilized in other techniques.

A — COUNTER TO A FRONT BEAR HUG

Fig. 30

Fig. 31

Fig. 30. Opponent grabs you from the front and pins both of your arms.

Fig. 31. Drop back with your right foot, simultaneously thrusting both thumbs to opponent's groin. (This should cause opponent to react by moving his waist back, thus giving you more leverage for the next move.)

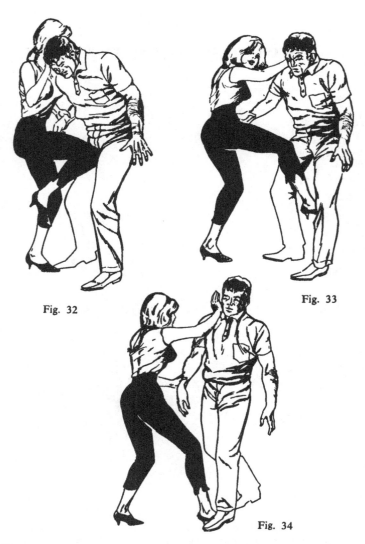

Fig. 32

Fig. 33

Fig. 34

Fig. 32. Drive your right knee into opponent's groin as your left hand grabs his right wrist and right hand keeps his head from hitting your head.

Fig. 33. Immediately kick with the knife-edge of your right foot to the inside of opponent's left knee.

Fig. 34. As you plant your right foot, (which could very easily be changed into a shin scrape and a right heel stomp to opponent's instep) strike forward with the heel of your right hand to opponent's chin.

B — COUNTER TO A REAR BEAR HUG

Fig. 35

Fig. 36

Fig. 35. Opponent grabs you from the back and pins both of your arms.
Fig. 36. Kick your right heel into opponent's left knee.

Fig. 37

Fig. 38

Fig. 37. Immediately use the same right heel to kick inside of opponent's right knee.

Fig. 38. Slide the knife-edge of your foot all the way down opponent's shin, continuing into a right heel stomp to the instep of opponent.

C — COUNTER TO A FRONT STRANGLE OR CHOKE

Fig. 39

Fig. 40

Fig. 39. Opponent places both hands on your throat in an attempt to strangle or choke.

Fig. 40. Force opponent's arms down with both of your hands as your right foot drops back.

Fig. 42

Fig. 41

Fig. 41. Maintain pull on opponent's arm as you drive your right knee into his groin.

Fig. 42. Cock, pivot (to your left) and drive the knife-edge of your right foot into the inside portion of opponent's left knee while your hands control his right arm.

Fig. 43

Fig. 44

Fig. 43. Pivot farther to your left and stomp back and down on opponent's instep.

Fig. 44. Immediately deliver a right back scoop kick. Using the back of your heel, kick up and against opponent's jaw. (You must keep your left knee bent in order to get force into your kick.)

D — COUNTER TO A REAR STRANGLE OR CHOKE
(TOP AND SIDE VIEW)

Fig. 45 a

Fig. 45 b

Figs. 45 a & b. Opponent places both hands on your neck in an attempt to strangle or choke.

Fig. 46 a

Fig. 46 b

Figs. 46 a & b. Step to your left as both of your hands grab both wrists of your opponent. (Squat low to make grab easier.)

Fig. 47 b

Fig. 47 a

Figs. 47 a & b. Step back and to your left with your right foot as you cross opponent's arms.

Fig. 48 a

Fig. 48 b

Figs. 48 a & b. Keeping opponent's arms crossed, kick with the knife-edge of your right foot to the inside of opponent's right knee.

Fig. 49 b

Fig. 49 a

Figs. 49 a & b. Plant your right foot forward pulling your opponent in with your left arm and push out with right arm to cause opponent's left elbow to break against his own right arm.

E — COUNTER TO A REAR FOREARM CHOKE

Fig. 50

Fig. 51

Fig. 50. Opponent encircles your neck and throat with his left arm.

Fig. 51. Have your right foot circle around and behind of opponent's left leg as you raise your right arm high, cocking your right elbow.

Fig. 52

Fig. 53

Fig. 52. Drive your right elbow back and into opponent's solar plexus.

Fig. 53. Pivot to your right and cock both of your arms high with your right arm in back of, and left arm in front of your opponent.

Fig. 54

Fig. 54. Simultaneously drive both hammerfists into opponent, right striking to opponent's kidney and left to opponent's groin.

F — COUNTER TO A FRONT LAPEL GRAB

Fig. 56

Fig. 55

Fig. 55. Opponent's left hand grabs your lapel.

Fig. 56. Grab your opponent's left wrist with your left hand, simultaneously kick his groin with your left foot and poke his eyes with your right fingers. (This maneuver is to acquaint you with doing two strikes at the same time thus utilizing the principle of economy of motion.)

G — COUNTER TO A FRONT TWO-HAND LAPEL GRAB

Fig. 57

Fig. 58

Fig. 57. Opponent grabs your lapels with both of his arms.

Fig. 58. Step back with your left foot as both of your arms travel inside of your opponent's arms, flicking the fingers of both your hands to opponent's eyes.

Fig. 60

Fig. 59

Fig. 59. Step forward slightly (if needed) as your left hand grabs and pulls opponent's right arm down. Simultaneously strike up to opponent's chin with your right elbow. In this way you will have two counter forces working for you.

Fig. 60. With left hand still maintaining grab, strike down to opponent's eyes and face with a right five-finger claw.

H — COUNTER TO A HAMMERLOCK

Fig. 61

Fig. 62

Fig. 61. Opponent's right arm pins you in a hammerlock as his left hand grabs your left shoulder.

Fig. 62. Shows your left arm inconspicuously cocking in front of you.

Fig. 64

Fig. 63

Fig. 63. Step back with your left foot and deliver an elbow strike to opponent's left jaw. In this illustration your efforts are blocked. Do not panic, but proceed to the next move.

Fig. 64. Step forward and to your right with your left foot as your right arm straightens and your right hand maintains a wrist grab on opponent's right wrist.

Fig. 65

Fig. 66

Fig. 65. Pivot clockwise twisting your opponent's right arm in the same direction with your right hand.

Fig. 66. Cock your left leg and left arm.

Fig. 68

Fig. 67

Fig. 67. Deliver a left side kick (with the knife-edge of your foot) to the inside of opponent's left knee.

Fig. 68. As you plant your left foot forward, simultaneously strike to the left elbow of opponent with your left forearm while still maintaining your grasp with your right hand. The counter force of pulling in with your right hand and striking out with your left forearm should cause a considerable amount of damage.

VII TECHNIQUES

COURSE III — (ARMED ATTACK)

This course deals with some possible defenses that can be used when you are confronted by an armed assailant. It must be explained that it would be unrealistic to assume that an armed attacker does not possess a tremendous advantage. The first choice should always be flight, if possible. But since this is not always possible, the following illustrations are some workable defensive measures. Types of armed attacks which occur most often are illustrated. It must also be pointed out that these techniques could also be applied if the opponent was not armed, but merely delivering a blow or a grab. These counters are designed to disable the attacker as much as possible.

A — COUNTER TO AN OVERHEAD CLUB

Fig. 69 Fig. 70

Fig. 69. Opponent is attempting to strike you over the head.

Fig. 70. Hop forward and to your left with your left foot as you block or deflect your opponent's right arm with your left palm. Simultaneously cock both your right foot and right arm.

Fig. 71   Fig. 72

Fig. 71. Deliver a right side kick to the outside of your opponent's right knee, thus buckling your opponent. Keep your left hand in a protective position as illustrated.

Fig. 72. Plant your right foot between opponent's legs.

Fig. 73

Fig. 73. Immediately deliver a right elbow strike to your opponent's mastoid or temple.

B — COUNTER TO A HOOKING CLUB

Fig. 74.
Fig. 75.

Fig. 74. Opponent is attempting to strike you in a hooking manner.

Fig. 75. Step forward with your left foot and block up with your left forearm, simultaneously delivering an upward reverse hammerfist to your opponent's groin.

C — COUNTER TO AN OVERHEAD KNIFE

Fig. 76

Fig. 77

Fig. 76. Opponent is attempting to stab you in an overhead fashion.

Fig. 77. Step forward and to your left with your left foot as your right arm begins to circle clockwise.

Fig. 78

Fig. 79

Fig. 78. Have your right and left arm follow the direction of your opponent's knife arm. Using your right hand, grab your opponent's right wrist and with your left hand grab your opponent's right elbow.

Fig. 79. Continue the action of your opponent forcing his knife into his right thigh.

D — COUNTER TO AN UNDERHAND KNIFE THRUST

Fig. 80

Fig. 80. Opponent is about to thrust his knife.

Fig. 81

Fig. 82

Fig. 81. Step forward and to your left on a 45 degree angle with your left foot as your right hand parries to deflect his knife arm away from you.

Fig. 82. If possible, control your opponent's right arm by grabbing it with your right hand and checking his right elbow with your left hand. Simultaneously deliver a right front kick to your opponent's groin.

E — COUNTER TO A FRONT SCARF STRANGLE

Fig. 83

Fig. 84

Fig. 83. Opponent places a scarf around your neck from the front.

Fig. 84. Flick with fingers of both your hands to your opponent's eyes as you step back with your right foot.

Fig. 85

Fig. 85. Grab your opponent's head with both your hands and as you force your opponent's head down, strike his chin with your right knee. (Your knee could also have been delivered to the groin.)

F — COUNTER TO A REAR SCARF STRANGLE

Fig. 87

Fig. 86

Fig. 86. Opponent places a scarf around your neck from the rear.

Fig. 87. Grab the scarf with your right hand as you turn your head to the left, and cock your left arm. Simultaneously cock and stomp your left foot on your opponent's left instep.

Fig. 88

Fig. 89

Fig. 88. Plant your left foot between your opponent's legs as your right hand pulls the scarf and your left elbow strikes to your opponent's solar-plexus.

Fig. 89. Release the scarf and deliver a right finger thrust to the eyes and a left hammerfist to your opponent's groin.

VIII TECHNIQUES

COURSE IV — (PERSONAL AND HOUSEHOLD ARTICLES AS WEAPONS)

This course will acquaint you with ways that some ordinary household or personal items can be adopted as weapons. Many household and personal articles are not utilized as potential weapons and an awareness of these articles and their uses as weapons may save your life.

The illustrations depict a girl using an umbrella as a weapon. A staff, which could be a broom, mop, or rake, is also shown. Whatever the technique, it must be remembered that other articles such as a purse, flashlight, iron, etc., can also be used as weapons. Discard ethical practices from your thoughts. If your life is at stake, preserve it in any way you can. You owe it to your loved ones, if not yourself.

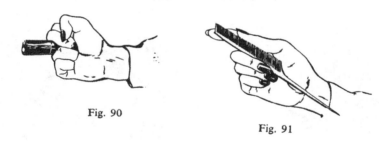

Fig. 90

Fig. 91

A — HOW TO USE A TUBE OF LIPSTICK

Fig. 90. This illustration shows the student how to use a tube of lipstick. One end protrudes as the other is held by the fingers and palm. With a thrusting motion, you could strike to the eyes, throat, temple, or solar-plexus.

B — HOW TO USE A COMB

Fig. 91. This illustration shows the student how to use a comb. The comb can be used in a slicing motion to the eyes, face, or throat.

C — HOW TO USE AN UMBRELLA

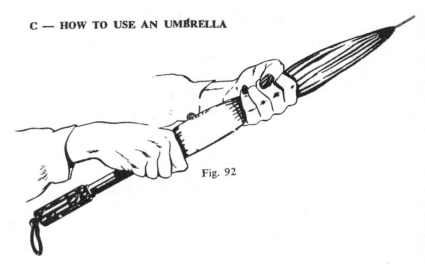

Fig. 92. Illustration shows the student how to use an umbrella. Uses of the umbrella are shown in the following illustrations.

Fig. 93. Girl holding an umbrella.

Fig. 94. Step forward with your left foot and thrust the point of the umbrella into the opponent's solar plexus.

Fig. 96

Fig. 95

Fig. 95. With your right hand, immediately strike opponent's left jaw with the umbrella handle.

Fig. 96. With the left hand have the point of the umbrella strike opponent's right jaw.

Fig. 97

Fig. 97. Kneel with right knee and have your right hand drive the handle of the umbrella up and into opponent's groin.

NOTE: The sequence of this technique can be interchanged so that a variation of the same movements can give you another working solution. For example: the following combinations can also be applicable, Figs. 93, 94 and 97 or 93, 96 and 97. Perhaps 93, 97, 96 and then 95 could be used. This example gives you a general idea of interchanging sequences. Use your imagination, remembering the principle of continuity and economy of motion.

D — HOW TO USE A BROOM OR STAFF

Fig. 98

Fig. 98. Girl holding a staff which could be a broom.

Fig. 99. Step forward with your left foot and thrust the point of the staff into you opponent's solar plexus.

Fig. 99

Fig. 100.

Fig. 101.

Fig. 100. Have the point of the staff circle clockwise and strike to your opponent's right temple.

Fig. 101. With your right hand have the other point of the staff strike your opponent's left jaw or temple as you step forward with your right foot.

NOTE: Again the above technique can be rearranged into another working sequence by interchanging the moves.

Fig. 102. This illustrates the point of the staff striking the opponent's left instep.

Fig. 103. An immediate follow-up with the point of the staff up and under your opponent's chin can be an effective counter offense.

Fig. 104.

Fig. 105.

Fig. 104. Shows opponent grabbing your staff with both of his hands.
Fig. 105. Deliver a right front snapping kick to your opponent's groin.

IX TECHNIQUES

COURSE V — (UNUSUAL POSITION—KNEELING OR LYING DOWN)

This course shows some methods of defense if the victim is caught in an unusual and often considered helpless position. In all of the situations illustrated, the girl is involved in some commonplace chore. In a prone position, she is sleeping or sun-bathing. While kneeling, she is involved in cleaning a floor or picking up an article. While seated, she is combing her hair or reading, etc.

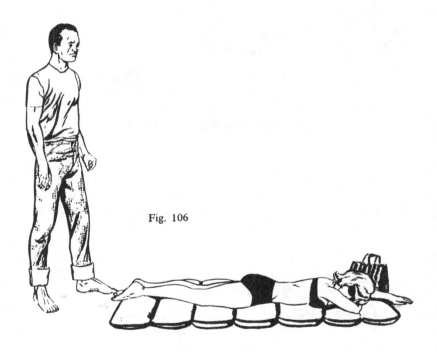

Fig. 106

A — HOW TO COUNTER AN ATTACK WHILE LYING ON YOUR STOMACH

Fig. 106. Opponent is approaching you while you are lying on your stomach.

Fig. 107

Fig. 107. Push yourself up with both of your arms as you cock your right leg and support yourself on your left knee.

Fig. 108. Use both of your arms to support you as you thrust a right back heel kick into your opponent's groin or abdomen.

Fig. 108

B — HOW TO COUNTER AN ATTACK WHILE LYING ON YOUR BACK

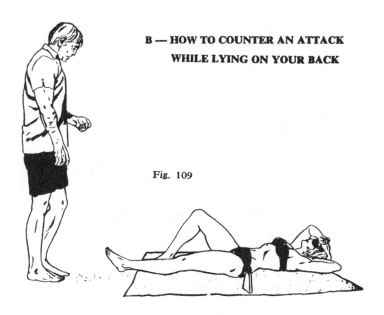

Fig. 109

Fig. 109. Opponent is approaching you while you are lying on your back.
Fig. 110. Roll over to your right side as your left leg cocks.

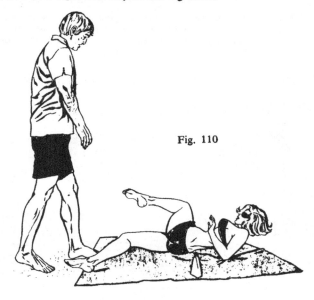

Fig. 110

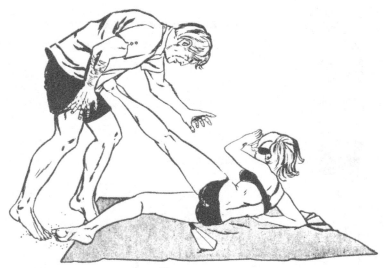

Fig. 111

Fig. 111. With the aid of your right elbow, thrust a side heel kick into your opponent's abdomen. His reaction will be to bend forward.

Fig. 112. Immediately roll over to your left side (supporting yourself with your left arm) and deliver a right side kick (using the side of the heel) to your opponent's left jaw. The kick should make contact right at the apex of your turn.

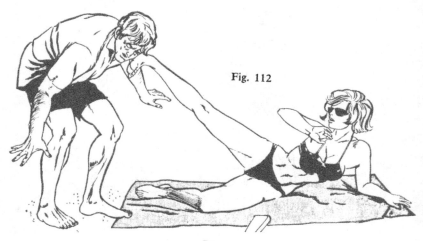

Fig. 112

C — HOW TO COUNTER AN ATTACK WHILE LYING ON YOUR BACK (VARIATION)

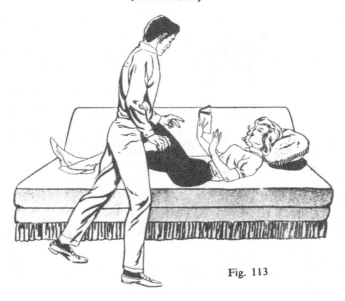

Fig. 113

Fig. 113. Opponent is approaching you while you are lying on your back on a couch.

Fig. 114. As opponent crouches to molest you, use your left hand to grab the clothing of your opponent's left shoulder, simultaneously delivering a right heel thrust to your opponent's chin.

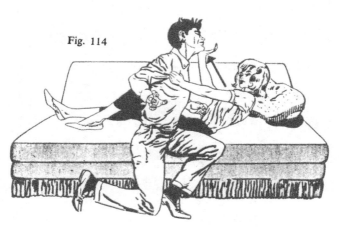

Fig. 115

Fig. 115. Grab the clothing of your opponent's right shoulder with your right hand and pull in with your left arm as you push out with your right.

Fig. 116. After forcing your opponent on his back, drop upon opponent as you force your right knee into his groin and your right elbow into his throat.

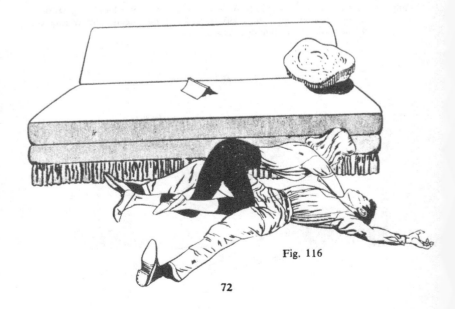

Fig. 116

D — HOW TO COUNTER FROM A KNEELING POSITION

Fig. 117

Fig. 117. Opponent grabs your shoulder while you are kneeling to dust the furniture.

Fig. 118. Raise up on your left leg (keeping that knee bent) and deliver a rear scoop kick to the groin (using the back of your heel).

Fig. 118

Fig. 119

Fig. 119. Cock your right leg while still maintaining a bend in your left knee.

Fig. 120. Thrust a back heel kick to the groin or abdomen of your opponent.

Fig. 120

E — HOW TO COUNTER FROM A SEATED POSITION

Fig. 122

Fig. 121

Fig. 121. Opponent approaches you while you are seated and combing your hair on a backless chair.

Fig. 122. Strike with a right back elbow to your opponent's groin.

Fig. 123

Fig. 124

Fig. 123. Immediately grab opponent's neck with your right arm and his hair with your left.

Fig. 124. Slip off the chair and kneel with your right knee as you force your opponent's head against the top of the dresser.

X HELPFUL HINTS & CONCLUSION

Keeping physically fit through exercise and proper diet is important as well as practicing the techniques. Practicing the techniques and kicks is, in itself, an excellent form of calisthenics, and useful in maintaining a trim figure. The reader must also be advised that a course in a good school of self-defense would prove beneficial and a useful adjunct to what you have learned from this book.

The following are TEN RULES to remember if ever you are attacked:

1. DON'T PANIC
2. DON'T FREEZE — BE FLEXIBLE
3. UTILIZE OBJECTS AND YOUR SURROUNDINGS AS WEAPONS
4. MAKE NOISES: SCREAM, YELL, ETC.
5. IF A TECHNIQUE STUNS YOUR ATTACKER, ESCAPE IMMEDIATELY; DON'T ATTEMPT TO FIGHT FURTHER
6. TAKE ADVANTAGE OF LIGHTED AREAS OR CROWDS
7. OBSERVE ANY OPENINGS
8. STRIKE AT THE MOST VUVLNERABLE POINTS
9. PLAN YOUR ATTACK
10. TRY TO KEEP YOUR ATTACKER AT A DISTANCE, IF FLIGHT IS NOT POSSIBLE

These are but a few rules; undoubtedly many others can apply. Nevertheless, it is our fervent hope that you will never find yourself in any of the situations illustrated. If you are not so fortunate, may the solutions illustrated work for you in obtaining the necessary results in becoming victorious in your escape.

For further information, catalogues, pamphlets, books, training films, tournament films, training equipment and other material pertaining to Karate and practical self-defense, write to ED PARKER ENTERPRISES, 1705 East Walnut St., Pasadena, California 91106. Application for Association membership is also available for those interested.

ABOUT THE AUTHOR

Ed Parker, a six-foot, devout Mormon, is one of the pioneers in the expansion of Karate in the United States. Although he first started Karate instruction in 1949 at Brigham Young University in Provo, Utah, it was not until 1956 after taking up residence in Pasadena, California that he actually put forth his great effort in the movement. Today he is the most renowned Karateist in the United States, being featured in widely circulated newspapers and magazines as well as being interviewed frequently on television.

He is President of the International Kenpo Karate Association whose membership roster now numbers in the thousands. Mr. Parker, in conjunction with other renowned leaders, was also instrumental in forming the United States Karate Congress, an organization encompassing associations of various styles of Karate. A great deal of the interest in Karate has stemmed from Mr. Parker's influence upon the TV and movie producers and writers, many of whom he has taught.

He has done much to educate the public as to the true nature of Karate. Samples of this can be witnessed at the International Karate Championships, the biggest and most successful Karate event of the year, held at Long Beach, California. This annual event which is produced by Mr. Parker, is an unquestionable display of Karate brotherhood where many men of different styles of Karate meet in friendly competition.

ABOUT THE ARTIST

Jim McQuade devoted much time and effort to the illustration of this important work, collaborating closely with Mr. Parker to insure the accuracy of his drawings. Born in Washington D.C., he served in a Marine reconnaissance company during the Korean conflict, afterwards attending the School of Visual Arts in New York City. Since graduation he has been active in both New York and Los Angeles in the commercial art field, having worked as art director of a book publishing firm and freelanced in advertising, magazine and book illustration. His most recent work has been doing paintings for pocketbook covers. Jim McQuade also illustrated Ed Parker's book, "Secrets of Chinese Karate," published by Prentice Hall. He currently maintains an art studio in New York City.

Made in the USA
Monee, IL
19 November 2024

70585296R00052